Amir Niza

The Bel

Methuen Drama

Published by Methuen Drama 2012

Methuen Drama, an imprint of Bloomsbury Publishing Plc

1 3 5 7 9 10 8 6 4 2

Methuen Drama
Bloomsbury Publishing Plc
50 Bedford Square
London WC1B 3DP
www.methuendrama.com

ISBN 978 1 408 17315 2

A CIP catalogue record for this book is available from the British Library

Available in the USA from Bloomsbury Academic & Professional,
175 Fifth Avenue/3rd Floor, New York, NY 10010.

Typeset by Mark Heslington Ltd, Scarborough, North Yorkshire
Printed and bound in Great Britain by
CPI Group (UK) Ltd, Croydon, CR0 4YY

Caution
All rights whatsoever in this play are strictly reserved and application
for performance etc. should be made before rehearsals begin to Judy Daish
Associates Ltd, 2 St Charles Place, London W10 6EG. No performance
may be given unless a licence has been obtained.

No rights in incidental music or songs contained in the work are hereby
granted and performance rights for any performance/presentation
whatsoever must be obtained from the respective copyright owners.

This book is produced using paper that is made from wood grown in
managed, sustainable forests. It is natural, renewable and recyclable.
The logging and manufacturing processes conform to the
environmental regulations of the country of origin.

A ShiberHur, Young Vic production co-produced with the Bush
Theatre and KVS Brussels. Part of World Stages London

The Beloved

by Amir Nizar Zuabi

21 May–9 June 2012

The Beloved is generously supported by Ramez and Tiziana Sousou.
Presented with the support of the British Council

With thanks to
Lyric Hammersmith, Young Vic, Anthony Newton, Guildhall
School of Music and Drama, Donmar Warehouse, English
Touring Theatre, National Theatre, Royal Court Theatre,
Stage Electrics, Catherine Kodicek

Cast

Young Son	Jonatan Bukshpan
Abraham	Makram J Khoury
Son	Rami Heuberger
Mother	Rivka Neumann
Wise Ram	Taher Najib
Wife	Sivan Sasson
Young Lamb	Samaa Wakeem

Creative Team

Director	Amir Nizar Zuabi
Designer	Jon Bausor
Lighting Designer	Jackie Shemesh
Sound Designer	Edward Lewis
Voice Coach	Emma Woodvine
Company Stage Manager	Lorna Adamson
Assistant Stage Manager	Claire Baldwin
Costume Supervisor	Charlotte Espinar
Floor structure	Weld-Fab
Set Builders	Young Vic
Scenic Artist	Richard Nutbourne at Coolflight
Dyeing	Gabrielle Firth

Creative Team – Production in Palestine

Composer	Daniel Meir
Production Manager	Eyal Vexler
Technical Manager	Firas Roby

Company

JONATAN BUKSHPAN Young Son

This is Jonatan's first professional production. He attends the Arts School, Tel Aviv, where his main subject is Theatre Studies. The course combines singing acting and dancing. Jonatan is looking forward to performing on stage at the Bush Theatre.

MAKRAM J KHOURY Abraham

International Work:

Theatre includes: *In The Penal Colony* (ShiberHur/Young Vic); *11 and 12* (Barbican-Bouff de Nord; *Al Jidaria* (National Palestinian Theatre). Films credits include: *Candies, Inheritance, Miral, Carmel, Italians, Lemon Tree, Munich, Forgiveness, Free Zone, The Syrian Bride, The Body, Galilee Wedding, The Three lost Jewels, Cantique de Pierre.* Television credits include: *The House of Saddam, The West Wing.*

RAMI HEUBERGER Son

Theatre credits include: *Hamlet, Macbeth, Three Sisters, Miss Julie, Taatuon* (The Kameri Theatre Of Tel-Aviv); *Summer And Smoke* (Bear Sheeba Theatre); *Hametz, Shivaa, Popcorn* (Beit Lesin Theatre); *One Flew Over The Cukoo's Nest, Waiting For Godot, Black Box, A Period Of Adjustment, Anna Karenina* (Habima The National Theatre Of Israel). Directing and acting credits include: *Scenes From Marriage,The Seagull, O Go My Man, Elling* (Habima The National Theatre Of Israel). Television includes: *The Kameri Quintet, In Treatment, Les Burguiane, The Priminister's Child's Grandmother Project.* Film credits include: *Snow In August, Letters From America, Schindlers List, Dogs Do Not Bark In Green Light, Dawn, Actors, X Explosion.*

TAHER NAJIB Wise Ram

Theatre credits includes: *I am Yusuf and This is My Brother* and *In the Penal Colony* (Shiber Hur/ Young Vic); *Damocles Sword, Forced Landing, The Thing* (Palestinian National theatre in Jerusalem); *Azir Salem* (Al-Kassaba theatre in Ramalla); *Peer Gynt* (Hebrew Theatre in Jaffa); *The Screens* (Habima Theatre); *Salome* (Hamaabada Theatre). Film credits include: *The Olive Harvest, The Moon, Sinking, A journey of Prostitute* and *I Frank*

In 2005 Taher participated in The Royal Court's international residency for playwrights. His writing credits include *In Spitting Distance, Both upon a time, Sea Wall.*

RIVKA NEUMANN Mother

Theatre credits include: *Romeo And Juliet, The House Of Bernarda Alba, Tis Pity She's A Whore* (Bier Sheva Theatre); *Top Girls, Measure For Measure, The Lost Women Of Troy, The House Of Bernarda Alba, Wild Honey, Three Sisters* (The Cameri Theatre); *Alice In Wonderland, The Screens* (Habima Theatre). Film credits include: *Berlin Jerusalem, Life Acording to Agfa, An Electric Blanket Named Moshe, The 92 minutes of Mr. Baum, Jesus.*

SIVAN SASSON Wife

Theatre credits include: *Servant of Two Masters, La Guerre Comme La Guerre, The Shape of Things, Alice in Wonderland, The Sunshine Boys, Perfect Wedding, The Vagina Monologues, August: Osage County, The 39 Steps* (Habina National Theatre of Israel), *Mr Kolpert (Tmuna Theatre Fringe).* Film credits include: *Walk on Water*

SAMAA WAKEEM Young Lamb

Theatre credits include: *Olive Harvest* (Saraia theatre – Jaffa), *I am Yusuf and this Is My Brother* (ShiburHur/Young Vic), *Belebelebel* (Al Midan Haifa, Haifa). Dance includes: *Love is My Religion*, *The Biography* and *the March* (rimaz dance company-Palestine), *I Remember* (Al Midan Haifa, Haifa).

Creatives

AMIR NIZAR ZUABI Playwright and Director

Amir Nizar Zuabi is the Artistic Director of ShiburHur. Writing and directing credits include *I am Yusuf and This is my Brother*, *In the Penal Colony*, *Alive From Palestine*; (ShiburHur/Young Vic). Other work includes: *Samson and Delilah* (Flanders Opera, Antwerp) and a dramatisation of the epic poem *Jidarriya* by Palestinian poet Mahmoud Darwish (Edinburgh International Festival, Bouffes du Nord and world tour). Further directing credits include: *A Comedy of Errors* (RSC as part of the World Shakespeare Festival)

JON BAUSOR Designer

Jon trained at Oxford University and on the Motley Theatre Design course. He is an associate artist of the RSC.

Recent theatre credits include: *The Tempest, Twelfth Night, Comedy of Errors, Winters Tale. King Lear* (RSC); *Ghost Stories* (Duke of Yorks, London/ Panasonic, Toronto); KURSK (shortlisted Best Design Evening Standard awards- Sound and Fury/ Young Vic/ Sydney Opera House); and *Lord of The Flies* (shortlisted Best Design Evening Standard Awards- Regents Park Open Air Theatre). Other theatre design includes: *The Birthday Party* (Lyric Hammersmith); *Water, Three Sisters* (Filter/ Lyric); *Terminus* (Abbey Theatre, Dublin/ Melbourne/ New York), *Julius Caesar* (Abbey Theatre, Dublin); *No Wise Men* (Peepolykus/ Liverpool Playhouse- winner Best Design Liverpool Daily Post); *Scenes from the Back of Beyond* (Royal Court); *Sanctuary* (National Theatre) *The Soldiers Tale* (Old Vic); *I am Yusuf and this is my Brother* (ShiburHur, Palestine/ Young Vic, London). Opera design credits include: *The Knot Garden* (Theatre an der Wien, Vienna); *Queen of Spades* (Festival Theatre, Edinburgh); *The Lighthouse* (Montepulciano); *The Human Comedy* (Young Vic). Design for Dance includes: *Blood Wedding* (Finnish National Ballet); *Pleasure's Progress, Ghosts,* (Royal Opera House); *A Tale of Two Cities* (Northern Ballet Theatre); *Scribblings* (Rambert); *Firebird,* (Bern Ballet, Switzerland); *Mixtures* (English National Ballet), *Wonderland* (Gallim Dance, BAC New York)

Jon is designing the Opening Ceremony of the Paralympic Games in London on 28th August 2012 at the Olympic Stadium.

EDWARD LEWIS Sound Designer

Edward studied Music at Oxford University and subsequently trained as a composer and sound designer at the Bournemouth Media School. He works in theatre, film, television and radio. He has recently been nominated for several Off West End Theatre Awards, and films he has recently worked on have won several awards at the LA International Film Festival and Filmstock International Film Festival.

Theatre credits include: *Gravity* (Birmingham Rep Theatre); *On The Rocks, Amongst Friends* and *Darker Shores* (Hampstead Theatre); *Slowly, Hurts Given and Received* and *Apple Pie* (Riverside Studios); *Measure For Measure* (Cardiff Sherman); *Emo* (Bristol Old Vic and Young Vic); *Once Upon A Time in Wigan* and *65 Miles* (Paines Plough / Hull Truck Theatre); *Krapp's Last Tape* and *Spoonface Steinberg* (Hull Truck); *The Shallow End* (Southwark Playhouse); *I Am Falling* (Sadler's Wells & The Gate, Notting Hill); *Orpheus and Eurydice* and *Quartet* (Old Vic Tunnels); *The Stronger, The Pariah, Boy With A Suitcase, Le Marriage* and *Meetings* (The Arcola); *Hedda* and *Breathing Irregular* (The Gate, Notting Hill); *Madness In Valencia* (Trafalgar Studios); *The Madness Of George III* and *Macbeth* (National Tours); *Othello* (Rose Theatre, Bankside); *Knives In Hens* (Battersea Arts Centre); *Personal Enemy* (White Bear & New York); *Accolade, Rigor Mortis, Fog, Don Juan Comes Back From The War, Perchance To Dream, Drama At Inish, In The Blood, The December Man, Beating Heart Cadaver, Blue Surge, The American Clock, His Greatness, Portraits* and *Mirror Teeth* (Finborough Theatre), as well as on the Arden Project for the Old Vic and the Vibrant season at the Finborough Theatre.

DANIEL MEIR Composer

Daniel is a composer and sound designer currently living in Tel Aviv, specializing in original music and sound design for video art, documentaries, film, and theater.

He has been working with critically acclaimed video artists and film makers from around the world. Notably, he has collaborated on works featured in the Venice Biennale and on the Oscar nominee and Cannes winning film. Film and documentary credits include: *Sharqiya, Cinema Jenin, Footnote – He'arat Shulaim, Lullbay To My Father, My Lovely Sister, My Australia, Dr. Pomerantz*. Video Art includes: *The Curator, Zamach – Assassination, Spies, Pioneer Tree,*

Gold Diamonds, Kosher Butcher, Uzi, Entartete Kunst Lebt, Leap Of Faith, Still Burning, 1000 Stars.

JACKIE SHEMESH Lighting Designer

Jackie designs for dance, theatre, opera and music. She studied at the Jerusalem School of Visual Theatre.

Theatre and opera credits include: *In the Penal Colony* (ShiburHur/ Young Vic); *As You Like It* (Curve Theatre, Leicester); *Ramayana* (Lyric Hammersmith); *In Spitting Distance* (The Rucab project); *The Hound of The Baskervilles* (WYP Leeds, Duchess theatre West End); *What we did to Weinstein* (Menier theatre); *Santé* (London Symphonic Orchestra); *From Canyons to Stars* (Hamburg Symphonic Orchestra). Dance works include: *Girl A* (Scottish Dance Theatre); *Lunatic* (National Dance Company Wales); *Habayta* (Nigel Charnock for Uzes Dance festival France);*Hungry Ghosts, It Needs Horses* (Lost Dog); *Dear Body, LOL* (Protein Dance); *Big In Bombay* (Dorky Park Berlin); Various pieces for the Bathsheva Ensemble years 1995–2005.

EMMA WOODVINE Voice Coach

Emma trained at Guildhall School of Music and Drama.

For the Young Vic: *I am Yusuf and This is My Brother, After Miss Julie.* Other theatre includes: *Noises Off* (Old Vic); *Macbeth, 'Tis Pity She's A Whore* (Cheek by Jowl); *Othello* (Sheffield Crucible); *GHOST the Musical* (Piccadilly Theatre); *11 and 12, The School for Scandal* (Barbican); *Breakfast at Tiffany's* (Theatre Royal Haymarket); *The Fastest Clock in the Universe* (Hampstead Theatre); *As You Like it* (Watford Palace Theatre); *After Miss Julie* (Young Vic). Television includes: *Christopher and his Kind* (BBC2).

ShiberHur

ShiberHur – [Shib-ër-Hûhr] 'an inch of freedom'

A compound of **Shiber** (an Ottoman measuring unit equal to an open palm) and **Hur** (Arabic for 'free').

ShiberHur is a new independent Palestinian theatre company based in Haifa and dedicated to producing the very best of contemporary and classical theatre for audiences across Palestine and abroad.

In 2008 a group of leading theatre practitioners, led by Amir Nizar Zuabi, founded ShiberHur to create a truly independent space where they can create high standard theatre. ShiberHur is an emerging and constantly evolving ensemble of performers and collaborators. Our mission is to break new ground, broaden access to theatre, generate new loyal audiences and foster a love for quality theatre in Palestine.

About the Bush

The Bush Theatre is a world-famous home for new plays and an internationally renowned champion of playwrights and artists. Since its inception in 1972, the Bush has pursued its singular vision of discovery, risk and entertainment from a distinctive corner of West London. Now located in a recently renovated library building on the Uxbridge Road in the heart of Shepherds Bush, the theatre houses a 144-seat auditorium, rehearsal rooms and a lively café bar.

www.bushtheatre.co.uk

bushgreen

bushgreen is a social-networking website for people in theatre to connect, collaborate and publish plays in innovative ways. Our mission is to connect playwrights with theatre practitioners and plays with producers, to promote best practice and inspire the creation of exciting new theatre.

bushgreen allows members to:

→ Submit plays directly to the Bush for our team to read and consider for production

→ Connect with other writers, directors, producers and theatres

→ Publish scripts online so more people can access your work

→ Read scripts from hundreds of new playwrights

There are thousands of members and hundreds of plays on the site.

To join, log on to
www.bushgreen.org

THANK YOU
TO OUR SUPPORTERS

The Bush Theatre would like to extend a very special 'Thank You' to the following Patrons, Corporate Supporters and Trusts & Foundations whose valuable contributions continue to help us nurture, develop and present some of the brightest new literary stars and theatre artists.

LONE STAR
Gianni Alen-Buckley
Michael Alen-Buckley
Francois & Julie Buclez
Siri & Rob Cope
Jonathan Ford & Susannah Herbert
Catherine Johnson
Caryn Mandabach
Miles Morland
Lady Susie Sainsbury
James & Virginia Turnbull
Nicholas & Francesca Whyatt

HANDFUL OF STARS
Anonymous
Micaela & Chris Boas
Jim Broadbent
Clyde Cooper
Blake & Michael Daffey
David & Alexandra Emmerson
Catherine Faulks
Chris & Sofia Fenichell
Christopher Hampton
Douglas Kennedy
Mark & Sophie Lewisohn
Eugenie White & Andrew Loewenthal
Adrian & Antonia Lloyd
Mounzer & Beatriz Nasr
Georgia Oetker
Claudia Rossler
Naomi Russell
Charles & Emma Sanderson
Eva Sanchez-Ampudia & Cyrille Walter
Joana & Henrik Schliemann
Jon & NoraLee Sedmak
Larus Shields
John & Amelia Winter

RISING STARS
Anonymous
Nick Balfour
Tessa Bamford
David Bernstein & Sophie Caruth
Simon Berry
John Bottrill
David Brooks
Karen Brost
Maggie Burrows
Clive Butler
Matthew Byam Shaw
Benedetta Cassinelli
Tim & Andrea Clark
Claude & Susie Cochin de Billy
Angela Cole
Matthew Cushen
Irene Danilovich
Michael & Marianne de Giorgio
Yvonna Demczynska
Judy Cummins & Karen Doherty
Ruth East
Charles Emmerson
Jane & David Fletcher

RISING STARS CONTINUED
Lady Antonia Fraser
Vivien Goodwin
Sarah Griffin
Hugh & Sarah Grootenhuis
Mr & Mrs Jan Gustafsson
Martin & Melanie Hall
Sarah Hall
Hugo & Julia Heath
Roy Hillyard
Urs & Alice Hodler
Bea Hollond
Simon Johnson
Ann & Ravi Joseph
Davina & Malcolm Judelson
Paul & Cathy Kafka
Rupert Jolley & Aine Kelly
Kristen Kennish
Tarek & Diala Khlat
Heather Killen
Sue Knox
Neil LaBute
Isabella Macpherson
Peter & Bettina Mallinson
Charlie & Polly McAndrew
Michael McCoy
Judith Mellor
Roger Miall
David & Anita Miles
Caro Millington
Pedro & Carole Neuhaus
Kate Pakenham
Mark & Anne Paterson
Julian & Amanda Platt
Lila Preston
Radfin Courier Service
Kirsty Raper
Clare Rich
Joanna Richards
Sarah Richards
Robert Rooney
Damian Rourke
Karen Scofield & LUCZA
Russ Shaw & Lesley Hill
Saleem & Alexandra Siddiqi
Melanie Slimmon
Brian Smith
William Smith-Bowers
Sebastian & Rebecca Speight
Nick Starr
Andrew & Emma Sutcliffe
The Uncertainty Principle
Ed Valzey
The van Tulleken family
Francois & Arelle von Hurter
Hilary Vyse & Mark Ellis
Trish Wadley
Amanda Waggott
Dame Harriet Walter
Edward Wild
Peter Wilson-Smith & Kat Callo
Alison Winter

CORPORATE SUPPORTERS

SPOTLIGHT
John Lewis, Park Royal

LIGHTBULB
The Agency (London) Ltd
AKA
Mozzo Coffee & La Marzocco
Talk Talk Ltd

The Bush would also like to thank **Markson Pianos, Westfield** and **West 12 Shopping & Leisure Centre**

TRUSTS AND FOUNDATIONS

The Andrew Lloyd Webber Foundation
The Daisy Trust
The D'Oyly Carte Charitable Trust
EC&O Venues Charitable Trust
The Elizabeth & Gordon Bloor Charitable Foundation
Foundation for Sport and the Arts
Garfield Weston Foundation
Garrick Charitable Trust
The Gatsby Charitable Foundation
The Goldsmiths' Company
The Grocers' Charity
The Harold Hyam Wingate Foundation
Jerwood Charitable Foundation
The John Thaw Foundation
The Laurie & Gillian Marsh Charitable Trust
The Leverhulme Trust
The Martin Bowley Charitable Trust
The Hon M J Samuel Charitable Trust
The Thistle Trust
Sir Siegmund Warburg's Voluntary Settlement

PUBLIC FUNDING

Supported by
ARTS COUNCIL ENGLAND

putting residents first

If you are interested in finding out how to be involved, please visit the 'Support Us' section of www.bushtheatre.co.uk, or call 020 8743 3584

The Beloved

*To David Lan who showed me the mountain
and to my wife Sivan who pushed me up*

Characters

Young Son
Abraham
Son
Mother
Wise Ram
Wife
Young Lamb

Act One – Mother

Scene One

Mother *is standing near a window.*
She is anxious and frightened.
We hear sheep bleating. It gets louder and louder.
Abraham *and* **Son** *come in.*
A strange silence.

Mother   Where were you?

Abraham   Out, we were out.

Mother   I know that, but you've been gone for days.

Abraham   Not now.

Mother   Not now?
  Son, where were you?

Young Son   I can't say. I promised father.

Mother   Let me look at you.

She pats him on the head, then turns him round
examining him, lifts him up and, moving very fast,
takes his clothes off him.

Young Son   Mother! You're hurting me.

Mother   Lift your hand up. We need to take this off.

She smells the shirt.

Abraham   I don't know what you're looking for.
  Stop it!

Mother   Lift your leg . . . Now the other . . .

She takes off his trousers. **Young Son** *stands in his underpants.*

She keeps inspecting him inch by inch.

Mother   You smell of fire.
Why does he smell of fire?
What is that? Why are your pants wet? Is that?
You're a big boy now . . . You're a big boy, what
happened?
Look at me.

Young Son   I promised father I won't . . .

Mother   I know, sweetheart, but. . .

Young Son   I promised.

Abraham   Leave him alone.
Don't make him break his promise.
A man doesn't break his promise. Never.
Go feed the sheep.
They must be starving.
I can hear them bleating.
I heard them all the way from the cypress grove.
Three days with no food, they must be going mad.
Now go.

Young Son *doesn't move. Long pause.*

Mother   No. No sheep. Not tonight.
Go straight to wash, straight.
Then come back, I'll give you some milk.

Young Son *stands, not knowing what to do.*

Abraham   Do as she says.

Mother   It's OK, you heard him.
It's OK.

Young Son *walks off.*

Mother *waits until he is outside, then speaks fast.*

Mother   You took him to the mountain?
I told you, I hate it when you take him to the mountain.
I told you.
He's too small to go there.

It's too windy.
It's too dangerous.
It's too rocky and all the cliffs –
What if he got injured? – He'll get killed.
It's dangerous there, it's too close to the border.
The soldiers. The enemy troops.
The wolves? Did you think about the wolves?
He's our only child – now he's my only child.
You don't . . .

Abraham   He was with me.
He was safe.

Mother   I can't go through this again.
Not another time.

Abraham   I'm hungry. We're hungry.
And it's too late. We'll talk about it in the morning.

Mother   I sit here and my belly aches from worry.
I sit here and my head is full of wind
and my bones are blue.
For three days I'm a wounded mare
with a horseman of fear walking me in circles.
Three days.
You look at him – I see that there is no love in your eyes.
I never see you hug him – then, all at once, you take him
    to the mountain for three days . . .

Abraham   He's back. That's all that matters. You got him
back.

Mother   What does that mean: you got him back?

Abraham   It means we're back – and everything is fine . . .

Mother   I am his mother.
He is my skin.
He is my ribs.
He is my spinal cord.
I am his mother.
Why did you take him to the mountain? For what?

Abraham   A father and a son walked out to the wilderness.
A father and a son came home unharmed.
The father is hungry, the son is tired. That's all.

Mother   When you didn't come back I had that same
feeling I had . . . seven years ago when you took . . .

Abraham (*cuts her off*)   I need to feed the sheep.
They're mad with hunger.
Can't you hear that? We'll talk in the morning.

Mother   Talk now! I beg you. Let's talk now.

Abraham   They're eating the wool off each others' backs.
I wish they'd stop that bleating.
It's driving me crazy.

Mother   What happened on the mountain?

Abraham   It's the pregnant mothers.
They're frightened for their unborn lambs.
I wish they'd shut up!

Mother   What did you mean, he is back unharmed?

Mother *grabs* **Abraham**.
He pushes her away, then leaves.
She picks up **Young Son***'s shirt and pants, smells them, then folds
them, then unfolds them and smells them again.*

Scene Two

Young Son *comes back. He stands still in his underwear, trembling.*

Mother *does not see him.*

The Sheep appear behind **Young Son**.

Young Lamb *stays with* **Young Son**.

Wise Ram *comes in speaks to* **Mother**.

Wise Ram   I heard a voice, a clear crystal voice, a bleat but
louder.

I was grazing in the mountain and I saw them –
The father was walking in silence,
his son, a young boy, walking behind him,
carrying wood, a big pile.
And I saw a knife.
I hid behind a bush.
I tried not to breathe; I tried not to bleat,
my tail was shaking with nerves.
I didn't want to move.
They stacked the wood. The son stacked the wood.
His father gazed up at the sky, looking for sign.
No sign came.
There was a silence, just an icy sound, a knife being
    sharpened.
The father said: I had a vision. . . You understand? I had a
    vision.
The boy nodded in acceptance or fear, I couldn't tell.
The father helped the son to lie then stood above him.
The boy was very still.
The father was crying, he was moving very slowly,
    deliberately.
It started to rain.
They both looked up at the same moment:
was that the sign?
White thick clouds just like my wool floating in air.
Soft rain. Just soft rain – not a sign.
It started to rain.
My merciful God whose body becomes visible in white
    clouds
has sent no sign.
What sign? –
The man stood looking up,
ran his fingers through his son's hair with so much
    tenderness.
His son smiled painfully, a smile of acceptance.
He was crying, I felt like crying too.
Two drops of rain fell on my head,
two drops of salty holy tears.

I tried to wipe them away on my woolly shoulder.
That's when my horns got snagged in the bush.
I tried to pull them out, I couldn't.
My neck was twisted, I'd got myself in a mess.
I was afraid.
'Father, it's raining, we have to hurry,' said the boy.
'If you get wet, you'll get a cough'
'My beloved son,' said the father, 'my beloved son.'
And then: nothing.
He picked up the knife.
The boy made a noise – it sounded like a bleat.
He didn't want to – out it came.
Trying to be brave, trying not to cry,
but smothering his fear out came a bleat.
He became a lamb.
I understood his fear. I know this fear.
I bleated back – instinctively – a mistake.
His fear met mine – two bleats crossing in mid air.
I didn't want to bleat, I didn't want to – out it came.
Both turned their head – at the same moment.
They saw me snagged in the bush.
That was their sign.
I was there sign.

The Sheep exit.

Mother *turns around to see her* **Young Son** *standing in the door way.*

Young Son   Mother.

Mother   Come, I'll hold you.

Young Son   Mother.

Mother   Don't stand in the draft.
You'll catch cold.

Young Son   Why does father have a knife?

Mother   For the lambs, in spring, it's spring soon, you know it's spring,
you know what happens in spring, for the sheep.

He has a knife for his beloved sheep.
Everything will be good here. Look at me, beautiful boy.
Let me hug you. Come.

She hugs him for a long time, then lifts his hands.

Are these rope marks?
What is that?
Don't be afraid.
Tell me.
What is that?

Young Son   I promised.
Why does father have a knife?

Mother   He has a knife for the sheep . . . for the lambs.
What is that?
Lift your head. Keep still.

Young Son   Can I have my milk now?

Mother   Yes, sweetheart.
What happened in the mountain?
Tell me. What happened!
Here you go, fresh milk.

Young Son   When you catch a lamb, you need to do it slowly,
with great patience, so the rest of the flock isn't startled.
Walk up to it, pat its head, behind the ears,
leisurely, do everything leisurely.
Then put a rope around its neck and lead it away
as if you're taking it to graze on fresh spring weeds.
It'll follow you, it trusts you.
Take it far enough away so the rest of the herd
can't hear it bleating or smell its fear.
Patiently hug it, gradually persuade it to lie down.
Use no sharp moves.
Tie its front legs,
then tie its rear legs.
Talk to it.

Stories, prayers.
Whisper to it.
If you don't, fear will tighten its muscles and its flesh goes
    hard.
Talk to it.
Then raise its neck gently, so you look it in the eye.
Then with one sweeping movement, from shoulder to
    shoulder,
a deep, swift cut.
Now leave it,
it needs to be alone.
It needs to die alone.
Can I have more milk?
Mother?
Why does father have a knife?

Black.

Scene Three

Young Son *is asleep in bed.*

Mother *stands above bed.*

*The Sheep are standing very close to each other gossiping and
secretly.*

Young Lamb   You think she'll leave him?

Wise Ram   She will not leave him.

Young Lamb   She might.

Wise Ram   She won't. She loves him too much.

Young Lamb   She almost left seven years ago.

Wise Ram   Almost.

Young Lamb   Yes. She still blames him for that.

Wise Ram   It wasn't his fault.
    It was a war. The boy died in the war.

Young Lamb   He sent him to the army.

Wise Ram   No, no, no.
The army took him.
There was a war.
They had to take him.

Young Lamb   The father was happy when they took him.

Wise Ram   Not happy.
No man's happy when his first-born's taken away from
    him.

Young Lamb   He was proud.

Wise Ram   Yes, he was proud that his son is now a man.
Every soldier is somebody's child. He was no different.
It's been seven years and I remember him
as if it happened yesterday.
He was strong and very tall, that son.

Young Lamb   Very tall.
I remember he used to come back from the army,
his hands smelling of knifes,
always smelled like narrow metal.

Wise Ram   That was the smell of death.
That day he took his son to the border,
to give him to the army; he was dressed in his smartest
    clothes.
She stood at the window crying,
the father so proud of his son become a man.
When they vanished around the bend
she ran after them to call them back
but half way up the hill she stopped running
and just stood there, waving her hand in the air at
    nothing.
She never forgave herself for not running to the top of the
    hill.

Young Lamb   That's why she'll spend the night packing a
bag.

Good thing the war is over.
The young boy is saved.
He won't have to go.

Wise Ram   The war is never over.
Here war is never finished.
It's just resting.

Abraham *comes in.*

The Sheep run away.

Mother *jumps to her feet.*

Mother   Don't come closer.

Abraham   The brown sheep has a bad cut in the rear leg.
It must have got trapped. It doesn't look good.
It's a shame. I think she's beyond saving.

Mother   Don't come closer.

Abraham   Are you afraid of me?
I am your husband.

Mother   Lower your voice. You'll wake him.
He has rope marks on his wrists.
You tied him up?

Abraham   I did, I had to – but only because he woke up
screaming.
I had to.

Mother   Tied him – because he was screaming?

Abraham   I was afraid he'll hurt himself.
He ran, it was dark.
He started running towards the border,
he wouldn't stop,
and the mountain . . . the cliffs . . . the wells . . .
I had to tie him, he wouldn't calm down.

Mother   The knife?
You held a knife to him?
He keeps on asking about your knife.

Abraham   Yes, I held my knife but not on him.
It was dark. Thick dark.
We were on the far side of the border.
I heard soldiers. They were so close by.
I heard them sniffing the air.
I took the knife to protect him. To protect him.

As **Abraham** *gets close to her,* **Mother** *bolts away.*

Mother   Don't come closer.
His neck? The bruise on his neck?
How did he get the bruise on his neck?

Abraham   His neck? I don't know,
He must have done that to himself,
when he was trying to break free.
He must have scratched his neck.
I love him. He's my son,
my only son. The only one I have now.

Stops talking at once.

Mother   You made him promise not to tell.
Why? What are you hiding?.

Abraham   I love you but . . . sometimes you are . . .
He's a boy. He thinks monsters exist.
He believes in the tooth fairy.
He thinks sheep can understand him.
And you take his word over mine?

Mother   Lower your voice.

Abraham   He can't stay under your dress forever.
That's why I took him to the mountain.
I know you worry but one day he'll have to fight.
We live so near the border,
you know they come here raiding.

What will happen if he stays like he is,
with his big innocent eyes?
The soldiers will cut him up.
They'll rape him, treat him like a girl.

Mother   That's a lie.

Abraham   It's not. You know it.

Mother   Let's move.
Let's go live somewhere where there's no danger.

Abraham   There's danger everywhere.
He needs to be strong.
He needs to be a man.
I want him to be ready, to be tough
so when they enemy soldiers come next time he's strong.
One time I failed . . .
When war begins he must survive.
I won't lose another son.
I don't want to fail again.

Mother   That's what you said when the army took my first
boy.

Abraham   You . . .That's what you think?
I didn't want them to take him to the war.
I didn't want them to but . . .

Mother   You sent him. You let them have him
and you were proud, you were so proud.

Abraham   Enough.

Mother   You were so proud.
When you took my son and gave him away.

Abraham   Enough.

Mother   I see you look at him and search for signs of his
brother,
in his face, in his eyes.
I see you.
I see you look at him with cold eyes and it frightens me.

Abraham   Enough.

Long pause.

How can you look at him as if you never had a son before?
You give him everything, all the old toys, everything.
How can you forget?

Mother   He needs me.
He is small and fragile and he needs me and he is so alive
    and he needs me.

Abraham   I want that too.
I want to feel that too.
I hear you say,
'Don't walk with your hands in your pocket.'
'Don't take off your shirt in the wind.'
'Chew your almonds ten times each side.'
And I want that too.
but I can't find the words . . .

Mother   Shhh . . . I didn't mean . . .

Abraham   I want that.
I want to love him, the way you do,
but I keep on failing him.
I take him to the mountain so we have a day alone,
but he is afraid of me.
Avoiding my eyes, kicking stones.
My head aches . . . I want to sleep . . .

Mother   Shush . . . It wasn't your fault. I am sorry.
What happened wasn't your fault. Look at me.

Abraham   I won't take him to the mountain again.
I promise.
I won't . . .

Mother   Look at him. Sleeping.
I look at him and believe everything will be good.
Everything must be good.

Abraham   Every thing will be.
Don't let him ruin every thing.
To sacrifice him to God?

Mother *is startled but controls herself.*

He is just imagining it's all in his head.
In the morning everything will seem different.
You'll see, we'll all cuddle in one bed,
one family, one bed. Everything will be good again.
You believe me?

Mother   Yes, in the morning. Yes.
I believe you.
In the morning every thing will be good.
I believe you.
Shush . . . The sheep are asleep at last.
You hear?
Nothing.
Just the wind.

Abraham   Come to bed.

Mother   Soon . . . I just want to look at him for a while.
You go. I'll be with you in a moment.

Abraham *leaves.* **Mother** *goes to bed, her thoughts galloping.*
Tears a long stretch of the blanket, wraps it around her hand.
Gets a bag from under the bed, organizes it and hides it.

Sleep, be patient. Sleep, get strong.
The morning is wide as your father's shoulders,
as your mother's bosom. Sleep. Be patient.

As soon as she is out, **Young Lamb** *gets out of the bed.*

Young Lamb   Your head is on a pillow of my wool
so you breathe my smell and hear my words.
We are the keepers of dreams.
We are the keepers of stories.
We keep the world in balance.
We walk in straight lines. We ask no questions.

We graze – but the grass has the flavour of steel
Because the more you eat, the fatter you get,
the closer you get to the butcher's knife.
That's why we don't ask questions – we dread the answer.
We died instead of you. Now live instead of us.
Run. Run, the first chance you have.
Don't look back, don't stop
until you collapse. You must.
Your father took you to the mountain.
He'll take you again.
Next time there'll be no rain.
Next time there'll be no lamb.

Young Son *starts up in bed. He looks frightened and confused.*

Young Son   Mother? Mother? Mother.

He sees **Young Lamb** *–* **Young Lamb** *bleats.*

Young Son *starts bleating too.*

Black.

Scene Four

The family is eating. There is a tense silence.

Young Son *is playing with the food on his plate.*

Mother   Do you like it?

Abraham   What?

Mother   The food.

Abraham   It's very good.

Mother   What will you do today?

Abraham   Work.

Mother   You'll go out with the herd?

Abraham   No.
It's really good – needs a little salt – but very good.
You should try some.
No?

Mother   So you are not going out?

Abraham   No. I'm not going out. I need to do things here.
The fence got broken. Some of the herd are missing.
Two or three. They must be close.
(*to* **Young Son**)
Do you want to help?
I'll let you use the saw?
What do you say?

Mother   He isn't eating.

Abraham   So he's not hungry.

Mother (*to* **Young Son**)   I cooked it for you. Lamb stew.
Why don't you try some?
Just a small bite for me.

Abraham   You need meat, that's what makes you strong,
That's what makes you big.
You're too thin. You need to . . . to

Young Son   Fatten?
Mother, is this the brown sheep?

Mother   No. No.

Young Son   I'm not hungry.

Mother *looks at* **Abraham**.

Abraham   It's really good. Can I have some more bread?
I think he should come with me.
A day out with his father.
I'll carry you on my shoulders . . .

Mother   It's too early.

Abraham   He can't stay in here all day.
I'll put you high up on my shoulders.
You can help me fix the fence.
Eat some vegetables. They're soft.

Mother   I let it cook since morning.
It's too early.
The trick is to let it cook a long, long time.
Maybe I can come with you?

Abraham   For what?
We'll walk to the creek.
They must be there – the sheep.
I'll let you build the fire.

Mother   He needs to eat.
Not today. Let him stay here today.
I couldn't find carrots. With carrots this is very tasty.
If you put carrots in . . .

Abraham   I'm going to finish my plate, then we'll go together.
Would you pass me the salt?

Mother   The carrots make it sweet but its good without them too.
Let me come with you so he's not . . .

Abraham   Alone with me?

Mother   That's not what I meant.

Abraham   It is!
I see you stare at me every time I go near him.
He tells you one single story and . . .
It's not real. He imagined . . . you imagined it the whole thing.

Young Son   Lift its neck, gently, so you're looking the lamb in the eye then with one sweeping movement, from shoulder to shoulder,
a deep fast cut.

Mother   Why are you saying that? Stop that.

Abraham *sits in silence eating slowly.*

He doesn't move, just brews up a storm.

Young Son   Now leave the lamb alone.

Abraham   It's all in your head, it's all in his head.

Young Son   Be patient. Let it fight for its life.

Mother   He doesn't know what he's saying.

Young Son   Let it move, that drains the blood, let the blood drain out
    every drop . . .

Mother   He's confused.

Young Son   Don't look at it now.
    It is its time alone. Let it be.

Mother   Stop that, sweetheart, I beg you.
    He'll hurt himself. Help me

Young Son   When it's down and motionless,
    use your knee to squeeze its rib cage.

Abraham   Stop him

Young Son   The air locked in its lungs will come out, one
    last bleat.

She hugs **Young Son***, tries to calm him. He tries to break free.*

Young Son   It's no longer a lamb, now it's – meat.
    Dead meat. Baaa. . . Baaa. . .

Mother   He'll hurt himself.
    Bring a rope.
    We have to tie him.
    He will hurt himself.

Abraham   What rope?

Mother   There's one in the sheep shed.
    Bring a rope fast! Please!

Abraham *runs out.*

She grabs **Young Son** *by both shoulders and shakes him, takes out the strip of blanket fabric. Her eyes stare at the door.*

Mother   Shhh.
  Be quiet. We're not safe here.
  We're going to run.
  You run, don't stop, we'll run until we drop,
  we'll run all night. I love you.
  Listen to me, don't let go my hand, squeeze my hand till it
    hurts.

She ties their hands together with the fabric.

  Sweetheart, what ever happens, don't let go of my hand.
  Whatever happens!

They go.

The Sheep come from under the table. They sit at the table, **Abraham** *comes back in holding a rope.*

He sees they are gone, drops the rope, sits to eat his food.

He starts to weep.

Abraham   It was God.
  God told me: take your boy, your only beloved son . . .

Young Lamb   It needs more salt.

Abraham   It was God.
  I heard a voice – the voice – it was God.

Wise Ram   Would you pass me the bread?

Abraham   Listen to me! It was God, not me!

Young Lamb   It smells very nice.

Wise Ram   It needs carrots.
  It's not the same without carrots.

Black.

Act Two – Son

Scene One

Son *in his late 30s and his* **Wife** *in her 30s. Both standing near a butcher's table. He is sharpening knives. She is looking out.*

Son   The truck crossed the border an hour ago.
They will be here soon.

Wife   Is it a big shipment?

Son   At least a hundred head.
I'll be working all night.
You look pale. Are you feeling OK?

Wife   I'm fine.

Son   You really look pale.
Maybe you should lie down.

Wife   No, I'm fine. And anyway, I want to be with you
before you go out . . .
It's just that I think that I . . .

Son   What?

Wife   I think that . . .

Son   What?

Wife   Nothing. I'll be fine.
Are you going to sharpen all these knives?

Son   Every single one.
I like to be ready – when they come.
It's going to take me all night.

Wife   Move. Let me help.

Son   Just be careful not to hurt yourself.

Wife   You be careful I don't hurt you.

Son   You won't. You love me too much.

Wife   I do.

They sharpen knives slowly.

Slowly they get into the same rhythm.

Son   I believe you can only do this with somebody you love.
Listen – we are one.

Wife   We are . . .
I can't breathe.

Son   What's the matter?

Wife   It's the smell.

Son   What smell?

Wife   The sheep feed.

Son   You can smell the feed?

Wife   Yes. I can hardly breathe.

Son   It never bothered you before.

Wife   I never smelled it before.

Son   So what's changed?

Wife   I can smell it now.
Thick moldy smell of hay . . . it smells like death.

Son   You . . . crazy funny thing you.

Wife   Listen . . .

Son   What?

Wife   When you finish
will you be sure to wash properly?
Last time there was blood all over the floor,
all over the sheets.

Son   I promise.
Sorry.

I'll do them all tonight.
The truck'll be here soon.
No time to waste.
They need to be at the packing plant tomorrow.

Wife   Don't kill yourself working.

Son   I'm paid per head, you know that.
The more sheep I do, the more money.
And we need all the money we can earn
if we want to have a farm of our own someday.
Anyway, I enjoy it, you know I do.

Wife   I'll never understand that.
Sometimes I think you hate them.

Son   Wrong. I don't hate them.
It's just something I'm good at,
I've always been good at.
The first time I slaughtered a sheep
I knew exactly what to do.
I don't remember where I learned it.
When I was small, we had no sheep
but I knew exactly what to do.
One fast swipe from shoulder to shoulder.
It seems natural.
It's as if I know what's going on in their heads.
I do it so fast they don't feel any pain.
I don't hate them.

Wife   Half the time I don't know what's going on in your
head.

Son   That's why you stay with me,
you hope one day you will.

Wife   True.
There's something I want to tell you.

Son   What?

Wife   I love you.

Son   What did you want to say?

Wife   I don't know.
One day you'll tell me what each of your knives is for.

Son   Generally speaking, this one is for cutting and this one is for cutting and this one is for cutting, cutting and cutting.

Wife   Stupid man.

Son   I love you.

Wife   So you should. You should.

They kiss.

Son   I need to check the fences.

Picks up all the knives he sharpened and starts walking out.

Wife   Wait. Listen . . .
Soon you'll have to start working harder.

Son   Again?

Wife   Soon you will have to work harder.
There will be three of us.

Son   I don't get it.
What . . .?
Are you sure?

Wife   Yesterday I was outside, I felt sick.
I was throwing up. But I was smiling to myself.
I'm sure.

Son   But I didn't . . .

Wife   You did. That one time almost five months ago.
We came home from your mother's birthday.
You were drunk and so angry, it just happened . . .

All the knives fall from his hands.

Son   You can't have him.
I am not ready.

We don't have money.
That's the truck. I can hear the truck.
I don't want him.

Wife   I want to be a mother.
Look at me.
I have to be a mother.

Son   They've arrived. I need to go.
I have to go out and unpack the sheep.
I don't . . .
We'll talk about this in the morning.
I don't want him.

Son *rushes out* – **Wife** *stands there.*

Young Lamb *comes in. She runs her hands over his back.*

Scene Two

Wise Ram   The world is losing its centre. It's out of balance.
These days everything's mechanical, a factory, totally
    automated.
They have conveyer belts now,
no human interference.
Gates open, gates shut,
unseen people push buttons that operate everything.
We are led to the blades,
then chopped, packaged.
Scrag, loin, chump, shank, breast, leg, shoulder.
Each part comes out chopped and packed
in styrofoam trays with see-through nylon covers in bright
    colours,
with a nice picture of a sheep in a meadow.
But those sheep never saw a blade of grass.
The only blade they meet is the machine.
But pictures help sell.
It's cost effective and efficient – words sharp as knives.
They – the humans – sleep at night feeling they're clean.

They're pure.
There is no blood.
There is no smell.
There is no noise.
But their dreams are hollow – their dreams are cold.
Their dreams fall on the pillow and ring like a coin.
We can't tell them their dreams
as they don't count us any more before they sleep, they
    take pills.
We don't float in the sky – we can't see the sky.
The sky is full of yellow smoke and when we try to float we
    sink.
Our wool's been replaced by nylon,
and the clouds have been replaced by drones.
The sky is full of drones – small metallic birds that people
    operate
sitting in rooms deep underground half way across the
    planet.
A cost effective and efficient way
to do to others what they do to us,
and sleep at night feeling clean, feeling pure because
there is no blood,
there is no smell,
there is no noise.
And they take a pill – one at least – so they can sleep
despite the fact that everything is so clean.

Son *comes in running. He is shocked.*

Wife   What's the matter?

Son   The table. Help me. I need the table.

Wife   What are you doing?

Son   Get away from the windows.
  All of them! They're all coming here.
  Bring me the bread knife.
  I had to leave my knives.
  The bread knife now!

Wife   What's happening?

Son   They surrounded me.
 They cut me off. I had to kick my way out.
 They came up this close.

Wife   Who did?

Son   The herd.

Wife   The herd?

Son   The sheep. The sheep.
 We took them off the truck,
 then the truck, the truck left.
 I walked into the pen
 and instead of running away like always,
 they looked at me,
 just stood there,
 all of them,
 looked at me.

Wife   Looked at you? I don't get . . .

Son   Yes, looked at me
 in a strange way . . .

Wife   Strange?

Son   Like they know me –
 as if they were looking for me,
 had something to tell me . . .

Wife   They know you? The sheep?
 You're shaking.

Son   Yes, the sheep.
 I separated one from the pack, a brown one.
 She didn't run away, she came to me.
 I led her. All the rest followed.
 The brown sheep told me – just as I was cutting her neck –
 'You can't be a father.'
 That's what she said.

'The world is not in balance,' that's what they said.
They want to come in.
Don't let them! Don't let . . .

Wife   I won't.
Look at me, it's OK, it's OK, you're just . . .
Sit . . . you are just . . . I . . .
What is happening?
Please, stop.

A loud bang is heard.

Son   They're trying to smash the fences.
They want to come in.
They said I can't be a father.
The thing inside you.
You have to stop him getting any bigger.

Wife   It's the wind, it knocked something.
It slammed a door. It's the wind.

Son   No, it's them.
We are the keepers of dreams.
We are the keepers of stories.
We keep the world . . .
I don't want to have a son.
They told me my blood is poisoned . . . because of the
   mountain.

Wife   We'll be OK, you'll be OK, just stop.
Here, have some water.
We'll be OK. Here, drink.
I love you. You hear me?

Son   I don't want him.
I don't want him.
Fall on your belly. Kill him.
Kill him. I can't be a father.
Not when the sheep are talking . . .

Wife   Calm down.
None of this happened. It's all in your head.

You're imagining it . . .
It's all in your head.
You're imagining . . .

He leaps at her and grabs her by the throat, a violent attack.

He punches her in the belly. She is on the ground but he goes.

Son   Don't say that.
It happened.

Wife   Stop. Please.

Son   They told me
I can't be a father.

Wife   Please . . .

Son   Don't say I imagined it.
Don't say that.

Wife   Stop.

Son   I can't have a son.
I don't want a son.
Kill it. – Stop it growing.

He leaves her.

She is on the ground, gasping for air, bleeding.

He starts to bleat frantically.

Son   Baa baaa.

From outside the sound of loud bleating from a herd of a hundred heads.

Black.

Scene Three

Inside the house **Mother** *in her late 50s is taking care of her son.*

He stares at a wall. Without moving.

Young Lamb   Baaaaa.
Seven years have passed and this place is falling apart.
There is grass everywhere.
There is grass sprouting out of the walls.
Grass is pushing up through the floor.
Grass is twisting out of the hearth.
We chew and chew
but grass grows faster than the living
and much faster than the dead

Wise Ram   We are all around on the hills, hundreds of us,
chewing the grass,
waiting for our shepherd to come out.
After what happened he stopped coming out.
And when she left him he left the grass to grow every
   where.
We chew and chew,
but the grass here is abundant like the pain.
Seven years have passed and our shepherd hasn't yet
come to herd us.

Mother   Have some milk.
Are you cold?

Son   No.

Mother   It's windy. You should fix the windows.
At least seal them with some boards.

Son   Tomorrow.

Mother   Yes, tomorrow.
The wind is coming up.
Aren't you cold?
Last night it rained.
You should wear warmer clothes.
Shall I bring you something warmer?

Son   No.

Mother   Drink your milk before it gets cold.
Yes . . . There's grass all over the doorway.
I tried to cut it – I can't do it alone.

Son   Tomorrow.

Mother   Yes.
You want more milk?

Son   No.

Mother   I cooked you a good stew.
Are you hungry?

Son   No.

Mother   When you were small you loved stew.
You loved to stand on a chair by my side as I cooked.
The first time I let you add spices you were proud.
Then one day you realized the meat came from our sheep.
You were sad. You left my side
and you didn't want any stew.
When you were small you. . .

Son   Tell me.

Mother   About what?

Son   About when I was small.
About my father, about the farm, about the land, the old
land.

Mother   There's nothing to tell.

Pause.

It's windy. You should fix the windows.

Son   Tomorrow.

Mother   Yes, tomorrow.
Have some milk.
Are you cold?

Son   No.

Mother   And the . . .

Son   Tomorrow.

Mother   I'll go get the stew.

Scene Four

Ram *talks to son.*

Wise Ram   We are the keepers of dreams.
   We are the keepers of stories.
   We keep the world in balance.
   Only after humans started following us did they start to
      understand the world.
   They are herd animals, people are, and need someone to
      follow
   They think they're our shepherds, that they lead us.
   But take a look at things – who follows who?
   We started taking care of them just after the descent from
      Eden,
   soon after the Big Bang.
   That's what we were sent here to do, this,
   and to become clouds.
   We nurtured them, gave them our wool to keep them
      warm,
   that is how much we pitied them.
   But then they invented knives and blades and –
   how should I put it?
   Our relationship deteriorated.
   But we forgive them, that is what we do, we have to
      because our forgiveness is the truth
   and it is as thick and as bright as our wool
   and it's what holds the world together.
   Without us the world would crumble to gray matter.
   When the last lamb's gone, that'll be the Day of Judgment.
   Yes, they tell themselves stories –
   Newtonian physics, gravity and falling apples –

but we can turn into clouds and float
detached in the sky every day.

Young Lamb *comes running in.*

Young Lamb   I saw her.

Wise Ram   Whom?

Young Lamb   The one who left.
The one who was pregnant – his wife.

Wise Ram   Where?

Young Lamb   She was outside the house.
I saw her creep up to a window.
She looked in – then ran away.

Wise Ram   Are you sure it was her?

Young Lamb   Yes. I followed her. She spent the whole night
circling the house
trying to find the courage to see him. To get in.

Wise Ram   She came to revenge her still born?
We have to stop her!

Young Lamb   No. I smelled something else.
I could smell her milk,
reeking off her skin, off her hair, off her breath.
She smelled white

Wise Ram   Are you sure?

Young Lamb   Yes, white – the smell of forgiveness.

Wise Ram   Or the smell glistening knives as they cut
through flesh.

Wife *comes in. She stands there unnoticed.*

Mother *sees her freezes both don't move for a long time.*

Mother   Would you like something to drink?

Wife   No . . . thank you.

Son *hears her. He is jolted but does not look up.*

Mother   Welcome.
  Why are you back?
  Do you want to sit?

Wife   Not yet.

Mother   Are you here to punish him for what happened?

Son   Mother.

Wife   No.

Mother   We don't need anyone.
  We're fine,
  me and my son.
  If you want to punish him for what he did when he was ill
  I'd say that's wrong.
  It was an accident.
  He was unwell.
  I'm sorry for what happened but . . .
  he wasn't well.

Wife   I want to talk only to my husband.

Son   Mother.

Mother   He is not your husband.
  You left him seven years ago.
  You left him when he needed you the most.
  You left him and broke him into pieces.
  He sits like this all day, my son.
  Now he is not your husband.
  I'm caring for him now and we're just fine.
  Inside he is good.
  He didn't want that to happen.

Wife   I know.
  I need to talk to him.

Mother   Because he's getting better,
slowly but he's getting better and it's unfair
that you come here and . . . break him into pieces.

Wife   I don't want that.

Mother   I have to protect him.
When he was small, I told him I'll protect him whatever
    happens.
I will protect him.

She takes out an old piece of fabric. It is almost disintegrating.

This kept us together.
When he was small, I'd tie my hand to his every night
Before we slept so he'd be safe with me,
so no one takes him.

Son   Mother.

Mother   I'll do anything to protect him.

Wife   I don't want to harm him.

Mother   I'll do what it takes. He is my son.

Wife   I don't want revenge.
I don't want to harm him.

Mother   Then why are you back?
Why?

Wife   I need to talk to him alone.

Mother   I don't trust you.
Anyway . . .
he needs to eat now. He needs his milk and his food now.

Son (*Shouts.*)   Mother.

Mother (*Pause.*)   Join us.
I did a stew with carrots, it's very good.
After you eat with us
you will leave.

Mother   Sit, if you want.
It's good, the stew, it's been cooking all morning.
Here is more milk, sweetheart.

Long pause. **Wife** *sits and eats with them then bolts up.*

Wife   Seven years I spent my nights wanting to kill you,
then kill the memory of you and of my dead son and I
    couldn't.
Spent my nights imagining how I put my hand in your
    blood,
up to the elbow and then spent the nights biting my hand
till it bleeds so I don't scream my pain.
It's very good the stew.
Then spent my nights staring at the ceiling hoping it will
    cave in on me, hoping that one second between 3:46
    and 3:47 in the morning
I will hear a crack and the whole thing will crash down,
suffocating me in a mix of concrete, metal.
Seven years all I wanted was to kill then die,
Kill you, then die.
Two and a half thousand days
and then the pain became comfortable.
It mixed with the water I drank and the salt on my bread –
until one day
I looked through the window and in the middle of the
    street
there was a lamb, a small lamb,
standing there eating the flowers growing on the
    roundabout,
cars rushing all around him,
but him calm, so calm, chewing flowers.
He looked at me, big black eyes
and I knew why he was there in the middle of traffic.
Two and a half thousand days.
That's how long it took me to forgive you.
And then at once all I wanted was
to see you, touch you, smell you.
I wanted to be home with my husband.

Mother   The wind blows so hard round here.
I'll go find a board to seal the window.

As she passes **Wife**, *she kisses her gently, almost unnoticed.*

Welcome home,
daughter.
He talked about you all the time,
all the time.

Mother *goes out.*

After a long time **Son** *lifts his head, then looks at the floor.*

Son   You can get the knife out.
I am ready.

Wife   I'm not here for that.
Look at me.
I know now why I'm here.
I'm here so you make me a mother again.
We'll start just where we stopped.

Son   I can't be a father.

Wife   I want you inside me.
I want new life inside me.
It must be you.
If I want to be whole and to live, it has to be you.
So we start where we stopped.
I need to become a mother.
We need it so we can live.

Son   I don't need anything.
I don't want to move. I want to stay like this, like a stone
until all this rots, until it all becomes dust.
The power to move, I can't find it.
I've been paralyzed since I saw his eyes.
I am paralyzed.
His big black innocent eyes look at me
and he was cold and purple – white
and his big black eyes look at me and say

    – I died for you, don't die for me,
my first son,
our first son.

Wife   Shhh. Don't talk.
It wasn't your fault.

Son   I did that to you,
to him.

Wife   It's not your fault!
Listen to me!

Son   It is.
I know it is.
It got into me, into my blood on a mountain.
I don't remember what happened.
I was ten, not more.
I don't remember what happened.
All I remember is rain and the smell of grass,
wet blades of grass close to my face.
My father hugging me so strong and the rain getting
   stronger.
And an icy sound of metal on stone again and again,
me wanting to run like wind, to run faster than the rain,
faster than my breath.
That's all I remember –
my father standing tall, his shadow a mountain
and the fear, the disease crawling in.
White fear. Covered with wool.
I remember the feeling: I can't do a thing, anything.
When the fear is climbing into me.
I remember its taste – like sucking on a metal coin.
I don't remember anything else,
just my father and the mountain.
Marwa? Moriah?

Wife   Give me your hand.
Can you feel me?
Can you feel how full of life I am, can you feel

this river of life?
Put your fingers in me.
Can you feel me?
I am a woman, a mother.

She gives him the knife.

Hold it.
That's how a man feels, a father.
That's what you need to feel.
Put your hand inside me.
You are my man, protect me.
Can you feel me?

Son   Yes.

Wife   Do you want me?

Son   Yes.

Son *stands up, starts kissing her.*

She holds his face and speaks very fast.

Wife   Sharpen your knife,
go to that mountain.
That's what you must do.
If your life was infected there in Moriah,
go find your father.
Get rid of the fear and the hate.
Hunt him down.
Put your life back in balance.
Put my life back in balance.

She breaks away from him. He stands holding the knife.

Then come back to me and bury your head in me.
Then come back and hold my hand when I give life to
    your son.
There's no time.
You have to make it all good
before I have our new son,
so he is born with no fear in his blood.

Son *starts to sharpen the knife.*

Wife *undresses slowly.*

Sheep come in.

Young Lamb   His mother packed his bag for him
with some bread and a rope.
She tied the piece of cloth around his wrist, a good luck
  charm.
She told him where to go
and asked him to tie the cloth to a branch of a little bush,
high up on the mountain.

Wise Ram   I know that bush. I know it well.
It's thick and your horns can get caught in it.
Hurry, we need the flock to gather and show him the way.

Young Lamb   I thought this would never happen.

Wise Ram   We need to go and lead him to the mountain.
All the sheep from around the hills, we'll walk with him.
We need to take him to Moriah.

Young Lamb   They say grass in Marwa is the sweetest.

Wise Ram   It is. It is the sweetest grass
but only because so much blood was shed there.

Black.

Act Three – Abraham

Scene One

Abraham *in his late 70s.*

On a mountain top; it's windy and very bare.

Son *is on his knees.*

Abraham *stands above him with a weapon pointed at him.*

Abraham   I don't want to have to shoot you.
  Who are you? What are you doing here?

Son   Nothing. Just standing –

Abraham   Are you – one of them?

Son   One of . . . ?

Abraham   The enemy! One of the enemy!
  Are you?

Son   I am not.

Abraham   You're sure?

Son   I am sure.

Abraham   I saw you crouching.
  What were you doing on the ground?
  Planting a mine?

Son   I was tying this ribbon to this bush.
  It's a good luck charm, I swear.
  I heard you cock your gun, I jumped.

Abraham   You armed?

Son   No.

Abraham   Good. Now charm luck somewhere else.
  This is the border.

Son   I don't see a border.
  Where is the border?

Abraham   Today – here.
The border is always moving
but the mountain stays in the same place.

Son   Is this Morwa?

Abraham   Morwa, Moriaha, depends who you ask.

Son   What are you doing here?

Abraham   Standing in the wind and waiting.

Son   Waiting for what?

Abraham   For people to leave this mountain alone,
for the border to melt back into the ground,
then the grass and sheep to come back.
Now you are standing in my place,
I don't like that

Son   Abraham?!

Abraham   Yes?
You know me?

Son   No.

Abraham   You said my name.
How did you know my name?

Son   You told me when we met.

Abraham   Liar! I never say my name.
Who are you?
Who are you?
I will count to three.
One . . . Two . . . I can smell the grass in your sweat . . .
Two . . . This smell of . . . Wool, stew, milk . . .
Three. It is you?
You came?

Son   Father.

Abraham   What do we do now?
You are so tall.
I was waiting for you.

What do we do?
Do we hug?
Do I hug you?

Son   Not yet.

Abraham   Right.
Let me look at you.
You are . . . If you are so big too much time has gone by.

Son   It seems like yesterday.
Grass was growing here just yesterday . . .
Don't you remember?

Abraham   What?

Son   The grass! I remember the grass green lush grass.
What happened here on the mountain? Do you remember
that ?

Abraham   No.

Son   Let me help you . . .
On the way up the mountain I was proud.
Look, father, look at this branch. Is it dry enough to make
a fire?
Do you remember that?

Abraham   I am an old man now.

Son   Fire likes to climb up!
Keep enough space between the branches. Fire likes wind
do you remember that?

Abraham   Son . . .

Son   I am not your son now.
Tell me.

Abraham   I don't remember.
You're too late.
I don't remember anymore.

Son   Was it here?
It was raining. I cried. I kicked. I called your name
but you were calling for God,
you were speaking with God.
You couldn't hear your own son.
Do you remember that?

Abraham   It never happened. It's lies.
It's all lies of weak, sick boy.

Son   I can feel it. I can still feel the metal – here.
Not all the time – when I drink ice cold water
and a week before the spring.

Abraham   None of this happened. It's all in your head.
You're imagining it . . .
It's all in your head . . . You're imagining . . .

Son   Tell me how it feels to hold a knife to your son's
throat.

Abraham   You made it all up.

Son   To see that he has peed on himself from fear.
To see his eyes look at you in amazement.

Abraham   The whole thing – a child's imagination.

Son   How did it feel?
I need to hear you say it.
That night – what happened?

Abraham   It's not true – it's not true.

Son   I can feel your knee on my rib cage.
That's true.
I can see you standing above me with your knife.

Abraham   It never happened.
You want the truth?
I took you up the mountain to make a man of you.
You were weak,
you were a little girl, spoiled, soft.

I tried to make you strong
but you were feeble and frightened.
You kept crying, you want to go home!
You were so afraid.
When we went home you told your mother lies,
evil lies that ruined our lives.

Son   I know what happened on this mountain.

Abraham   You don't, you don't.
You are full of confusions, nothing is certain in your life.
That's why you came here.
You're not certain what happened.
And you can't ask your mother because deep inside you
you know she doesn't believe you.

Son   Shut up.

Abraham   She hated you for making her leave her husband
and live like a dog in refugee camps.
She had to clean toilets to earn enough to feed you.

Son   Shut up.

Abraham   You killed her life. That's the truth!
What are you going to do now, lamb?

Son   Kill you.

Abraham   You? Don't make me laugh.
Your brother. He was a man.
You were pale, feeble, always crying, always weird
with your big eyes and your wild imagination.
You were never like him.
When he died in the war
my heart was cut out with a knife.
What are you going to do?
I asked you: what are you going to do, lamb?

Son *leaps on his* **Abraham** *they fight over the gun.*

Son *takes it and beats his* **Abraham** *to the ground.*

Son *ties him with a rope.*

Son   When you held the knife to my throat . . .
the lamb entered in . . .
I opened my mouth to beg for mercy
and the lamb climbed in.
Into me, into my cells, through every pore, into my bones.
The lamb came in – I became a lamb – a sacrificial lamb.
Something happened to me under your knife,
something astonishing.
I was no longer a human being.
I knew that at once.
I became a blend of clouds and ashes,
big black eyes, acceptance and submission.
I became a lamb.
I need to hear you tell me.
What happened that night?

Abraham   Forgive me.

Son   I will forgive you.
I don't have any hate – I am a lamb.
I don't want revenge – I am a lamb.
I will not harm you . . . I am a lamb.
I will forgive you.
Tell me why you did that.
Why did you take me there?
Say it.

He takes out a butcher's knife, starts sharpening it.

Abraham   Stop, son,
I beg you . . .
Do you know what you're doing ?
I am your father.

Son   Say it.

Abraham   Remember I taught you how to eat a nut?
Chew it carefully, ten times in each side of the mouth so
you don't choke? Ten times.

Son   Say it!

Abraham   I covered you in the cold nights. Remember?
I taught you not to run with your hand in your pockets.
Forgive . . .

Son   Say it!

Abraham   Stop – I beg you, stop!
I had a vision.
I had a vision.
Your brother was always there between us.
Every time I hugged you – I smelled him,
every time I looked at what I had I remembered what I
    lost.
I started hating that you are so beautiful and alive.
My first son, my beloved son who was sacrificed in war,
was rotting under the grass on the mountain near the
    border.
Then one day a brown ram looked at me and told me,
'Put your young son in the grass and take the beloved one
    out.'
He told me that I heard him.
He said that your brother is waiting under the grass for
    me.
Under the thick green. That's what he said.
When I took you to the mountain
I wanted to put you in the grass and take him home,
that's what I wanted to do.
I had a vision – it was a sign.
When we got to the top of the mountain
it was very windy.
We sat in a patch of grass.
You put your head in my lap and fell asleep.
I took my knife out, put it on you your throat.
And then I saw –
I saw your ear.
I couldn't move.
An ear – so complex, perfect, helpless.
Everything about you was malleable and burnished.
I didn't know anything could be so warm, so alive.

The knife was ready in my hand but
your neck, your lips, your tight shut eyes and your ear
shouted:
'Wait, wait. Do not harm the boy.'
I held the knife . . . up . . .
He was right, the brown ram, he was right.
I found The beloved one.
I found you . . .
Your head heavy on my thigh.
How simple is human happiness.
I didn't move. My leg went numb.
I sat there like a stone.
How simple was human happiness.
I saw the lamb again, he was bleating in the wind;
I moved.
Then you woke up and saw the knife.
And there was no way back.
Forgive me.
I was full of love for you. Forgive . . .

Son   You know I do.
But . . . I have no choice . . .
You left me half done,
I never trusted anyone any more.
I am a man – sheep.

Abraham   You said you will forgive – forgive,
I beg you. Go back . . . to your wife . . . Go back.

Son   If I want to go on living
I need to become human again, a man.
The only way is to lift this knife,
the only way is to tell you a story about a green pasture
on a steep mountain that was once called Moriah.
And then lift your neck, gently, so you're looking me in
    the eye,
then with a sweeping movement from shoulder to
    shoulder,
a deep swift cut . . .

I have to, father, so I can go home to my wife,
to my soon to be born son and be whole, be clean, be pure.
This must end here, can you understand that?
I need to leave the old land and its ancient names and its
 old stories, and leave you and leave the fear and go
 back . . .
Father? My father. I forgive you. Can you forgive me?
The only way to become a man is to hold this end of the
 knife.

A sheep comes on, grazing leisurely . . . One bleat.

Father *and* **Son** *turn to look.*

Abraham   Son. Stop. Wait . . . Look . . . A sign . . .

Son   It's not a sign.
It's just a sheep that came to climb into you
when you beg for mercy.
Shoo . . . Go away, lamb . . . We don't need you, lamb.
I've been practicing all my life.
One swift move from shoulder to shoulder.
I forgive you, Father.

Son *stands. The knife is hanging from his hand,* **Abraham** *and*
Son *look at it.* **Young Lamb** *bleats again – a long, long bleat*

Black.

Epilogue

Wife, *with a big belly, stands looking out.*
She holds her legs tight.

Wife   I can hear his footsteps on the thick grass.
He's hurrying down the mountain.
He is tired, he has been walking a long time.
His feet are wet, his shoes are wet from the lush green
 grass.
He runs . . . He walks, then runs, then walks, then runs.
That's how much he wants to come back to you.

I can see him standing half bent,
his thumbs digging into his waist,
mouth open, gasping,
trying to catch his breath.
But his breath is very fast,
it wants to be free and run,
run to us, to you.
That's how much your father wants to be home.
Just stay inside your mother for another week,
for another day,
just until the world is spinning in balance,
just until we see your father and his strong breath
racing down the street.
Who will be here first, your father or his breath?
Your brother was born white and had big eyes,
but you will be born with your eyes shut.
You will be born agile like an almond tree,
and your father will be there to give you a name.
He will hold you and name you.
He is running through the long grass.
Stay inside until the world is right.
Stay inside your mother.
So you are a man, not a lamb.
Stay inside your mother
stay
so the world will be good.

Black.